# NICK OF TIME

Words and Music by Bonnie Raitt

A friend of mine, she cries___ at night___ and she calls___ me on the phone.
I see my folks, they're get - ting on,___ and I watch their bod - ies change.
Just when I thought I'd had ___ e - nough___ and all my tears were shed,

Sees ba - bies ev - 'ry - where ___ she goes___ and she
I know they see the same ___ in me___ and it
no prom - ise left un - bro - ken, there ___ were no

wants one of her own. ___
makes us both feel strange. ___
pain - ful words un - said, ___

She's wait - ed long e - nough, ___
No mat - ter how you tell ___
you came a - long and showed ___

___ she says, ___ and
___ your - self it's
___ me I ___ could

still he can't de - cide.
what we all ___ go through,
leave it all ___ be - hind.

4

TYLER

DEBORAH FRANKEL

# N I C K
# O F
# T I M E

Management: Danny Goldberg & Ron Stone
Piano/Vocal Arrangements by Ed Conte
Music Engraving by W. R. Music
Production Manager: Daniel Rosenbaum
Art Direction: Alisa Hill
Administration: Tom Haydock
Director of Music: Mark Phillips

*Cover photo by Deborah Frankel*

*Photos courtesy of Capitol Records*

ISBN: 0-89524-440-3

*Edited by Milton Okun*

# CONTENTS

**12**
Cry on My Shoulder

**39**
Have a Heart

**30**
I Ain't Gonna Let You Break My Heart Again

**20**
I Will Not Be Denied

**8**
Love Letter

**3**
Nick of Time

**16**
Nobody's Girl

**47**
Real Man

**34**
The Road's My Middle Name

**51**
Thing Called Love

**44**
Too Soon To Tell

COMPLETE LYRICS AND FULL COLOR FOLD-OUT FOLLOW PAGE 23

Life gets mighty precious when there's less of it to waste.

Scared you'll run out of time.

I found love, babe, love in the nick of time.

*Repeat and fade*

# LOVE LETTER

Words and Music by Bonnie Hayes

Chorus

Work-ing on a love____ let-ter,                    list-'ning to a love____ song.

I'm writ-ing you a love____ let-ter,  love____ let-ter,                    with the

ra-di-o____ on.        (Ra-di-o,____ ra-di-o).     Hope you get the mes-sage, ba-by.

I know that you're____ gon-na let me in.____                                It's

weird   in your neigh-bor-hood.____        If  this  is  war____ then I'm____ gon-na win.

# CRY ON MY SHOULDER

Words and Music by Michael Ruff

*Pianists: Omit vocal melody

My_____ love._____

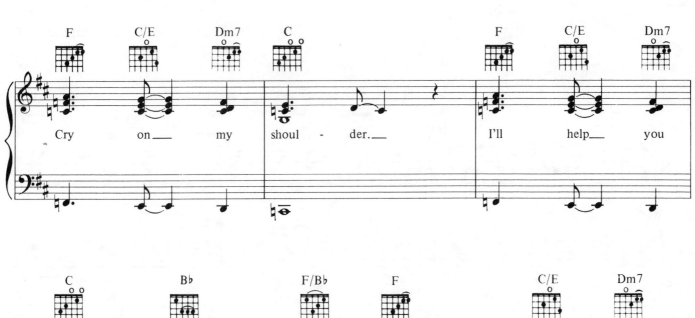

Cry on \_\_\_ my shoul - der. \_\_\_ I'll help \_\_\_ you

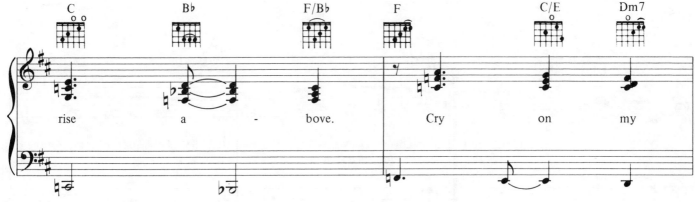

rise a - bove. Cry on my

shoul - der, \_\_\_ my love. \_\_\_

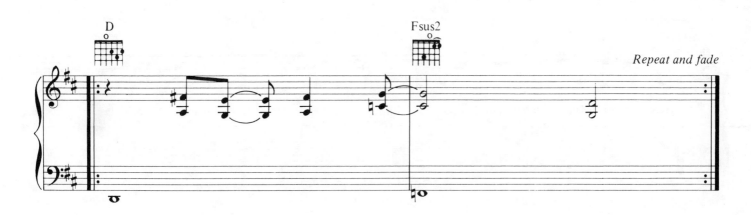

*Repeat and fade*

# NOBODY'S GIRL

Words and Music by Larry John McNally

***Additional Lyrics***

2. She shows up at his doorstep in the middle of the night,
   Then she disappears for weeks at a time.
   Just enough to keep him wanting more,
   But never is he satisfied.
   And he's left to pick up the pieces,
   Wondering what does he do this for.
   She's off in her own little world,
   She's nobody's girl,
   She's nobody's girl. *(To Bridge)*

3. She does anything she wants anytime she wants to
   With anyone you know she wants at all.
   Still she gets all upset over the least little thing.
   Man, you hurt her, it makes you feel so small.
   And she's a walking contradiction,
   But I ache for her inside.
   She's fragile like a string of pearls.
   She's nobody's girl. *(etc.)*

# I WILL NOT BE DENIED

Words and Music by Jerry L. Williams

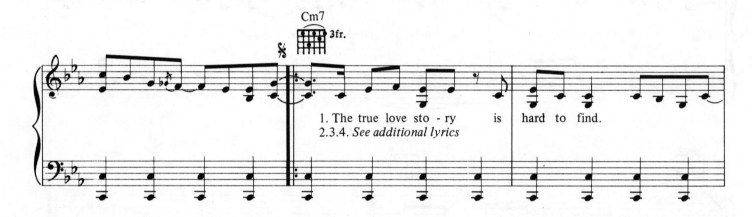

1. The true love sto-ry is hard to find.
2.3.4. *See additional lyrics*

Can't get no rest, got no peace of mind. They say you gave___ your

heart to me.___ You put me down___ and set me free. Said you're

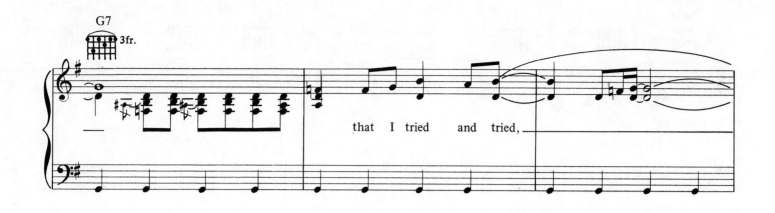

that I tried and tried,

but you just can't get e - nough.
So, you lied and lied

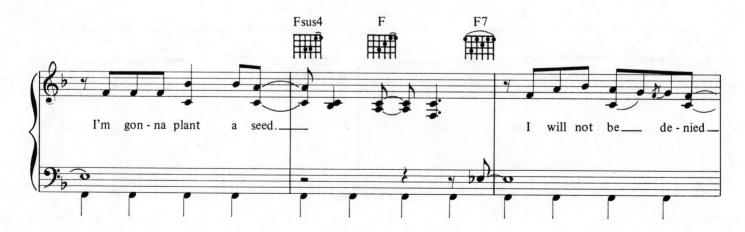

*To Coda* ⊕

and lied and lied. I will not be de - nied.

Fsus4    F    F7

Fsus4    F    F7

I'm gon - na plant a seed.
I will not be de - nied

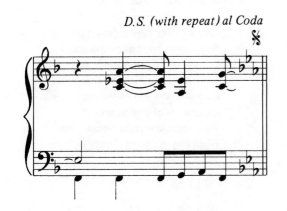

*Additional Lyrics*

2. You said you were the only one.
   Come in on me and ruin my fun.
   Leave me sittin' at home all alone.
   Waitin' on your call by the telephone. *(To Chorus)*

3. *Instrumental (To Chorus)*

4. It's a sad situation, yes, it's true.
   I can say it, baby, I'm through with you.
   It's over now and in the past.
   Gonna find me a man with a love that'll last. *(To Chorus)*

## NICK OF TIME

*Words and Music by Bonnie Raitt*

A friend of mine, she cries at night
And she calls me on the phone
Sees babies everywhere she goes
And she wants one of her own
She's waited long enough, she says
And still he can't decide
Pretty soon she'll have to choose
And it tears her up inside

She's scared...
Scared she'll run out of time

I see my folks, they're getting on
And I watch their bodies change
I know they see the same in me
And it makes us both feel strange
No matter how you tell yourself
It's what we all go through
Those lines look pretty hard to take
When they're staring back to you

Oh, oh, scared you'll run out of time

When did the choices get so hard
With so much more at stake?
Life gets mighty precious
When there's less of it to waste

Scared you'll run out of time

Just when I thought I'd had enough
And all my tears were shed
No promise left unbroken
There were no painful words unsaid
You came along and showed me
I could leave it all behind
You opened up my heart again
And then much to my surprise

I found love, babe
Love in the nick of time
I found love, darlin'
Love in the nick of time
I found love, baby
Love in the nick of time

BONNIE

RAITT

## LOVE LETTER

*Words and Music by Bonnie Hayes*

Sitting in front of your house
Light rain and an early dawn
Working on a love letter
With the radio on

Got my eye on your window pane
And I smoked a lot of cigarettes
Mercy, mercy, but love is strange
And you haven't even kissed me yet

We come to push
Push comes to shove
Shove comes to touch
Touch will come to love

Working on a love letter
Listening to a love song
I'm writing you a love letter
Love letter, with the radio on

Hope you get the message, baby
I know that you're gonna let me in
It's weird in your neighborhood
If this is war, then I'm gonna win

We come to push
Push comes to shove
Shove comes to touch
Touch will come to love
Love don't sit waiting
Love don't behave
Love's waiting in the car
In the pouring rain

I'm working on a love letter
Listening to a love song
I'm writing you a love letter
Love letter, with the radio on

## CRY ON MY SHOULDER

*Words and Music by Michael Ruff*

I know it's hard sometimes
And things seem larger than they are
But if you need to tell someone
That's what I'm here for

Cry on my shoulder
I'll help you rise above
Cry on my shoulder, my love

And in the world outside
It can be harsh and cold
But if you need someone
I will be here to hold you

Cry on my shoulder
I'll help you dry your eyes
Cry on my shoulder, my love
My love

I know it's hard sometimes
And things seem larger than they are
But if you need to let it go
Then you can call on me

Cry on my shoulder
I'll help you dry your eyes
Cry on my shoulder, my love

Cry on my shoulder
I'll help you rise above
Cry on my shoulder, my love
My love

## NOBODY'S GIRL

*Words and Music by Larry John McNally*

She don't need anybody to tell her she's pretty
She's heard it every single day of her life
He's got to wonder what she sees in him
When there's so many others standing in line
She gives herself to him
But he's still on the outside
She's alone in this world
She's nobody's girl
She's nobody's girl

She shows up at his doorstep in the middle of the night
Then she disappears for weeks at a time
Just enough to keep him wanting more
But never is he satisfied
And he's left to pick up the pieces
Wondering what does he do this for
She's off in her own little world
She's nobody's girl
She's nobody's girl

He said, "Before I met her I didn't love nothin'
I could take it and leave it, that was okay
She brings out a want in me
For things I didn't even know that I need"

She does anything she wants anytime she wants to
With anyone you know she wants at all
Still she gets all upset over the least little thing
Man, you hurt her, it makes you feel so small
And she's a walking contradiction
But I ache for her inside
She's fragile like a string of pearls
She's nobody's girl
She's fragile like a string of pearls
She's nobody's girl
She's nobody's girl
She's nobody's girl

## I WILL NOT BE DENIED

*Words and Music by Jerry L. Williams*

The true story is hard to find
Can't get no rest, got no peace of mind
They say you gave your heart to me
You put me down and set me free

Said you're deadly
Everybody said you was deadly
Guess you know he is because
Deadly comes in every shape and size
Deadly always takes you by surprise

You said you were the only one
Come in on me and ruin my fun
You leave me sittin' at home all alone
Waitin' on your call by the telephone

Said you're deadly
Everybody said you was deadly
Guess you know you always was deadly
Comes in every shape and size
Deadly finally made me realize
That I tried and tried
But you just can't get enough
So you lied and lied and lied and lied
I will not be denied
I'm gonna plant a seed
I will not be denied
Of the man and the love I need

Said you're deadly
Everybody said you was deadly
Guess you know you are because
Deadly comes in every shape and size
Deadly always takes you by surprise

It's a sad situation, yes it's true
I can say it baby, I'm through with you
It's over now and in the past
Gonna find me a man with a love that'll last

Said you're deadly
Everybody said you was deadly
Guess you know you've always been deadly
Comes in every shape and size
Deadly finally made me realize
That I tried and tried
But you just can't get enough
So you lied and lied and lied and lied
I will not be denied

## I AIN'T GONNA LET YOU BREAK MY HEART AGAIN

*Words by David Lasley and Julie Lasley
Music by David Lasley*

There ain't no use in me
Try'n to tell you how I feel
'Cause what I feel ain't what you're feelin'
I don't know what we did wrong
I just know if you come home
I ain't gonna let you break my heart again

There ain't no use in me
Try'n to find out where you been
'Cause where you been ain't where I'm goin'
'Cause if I ask ya where you've been
The hurtin' starts and it don't end
So, I ain't gonna let you break my heart again
No, I ain't gonna let you break my heart again, no

Tears don't become me
Pain ain't my friend
It seems like you enjoy my cryin', baby
You always said that I was strong
And I believed that you were wrong
Lately, God knows, I've been tryin'

There ain't no use in you
Try'n to kiss away the hurt, baby
'Cause it hurts where it's deep down inside of me
and it's hiding
If you decide you're comin' home
You walk in, it won't be like before
'Cause I ain't gonna let you break my heart again, no
Ain't gonna let you break my heart again, no, no

## THE ROAD'S MY MIDDLE NAME

*Words and Music by Bonnie Raitt*

I told you once the day we met
I wouldn't be your queen
Your little darlin', sweet coquette
Just wasn't my routine
You've been around enough to know
There's really no one else
When I hear that siren call, baby
I just can't help myself

I got to go
I hope you'll understand
I love you so
Want you to be my man

I hear it call
Sounds so sweet and plain
I got to go, baby
'Cause the road's my middle name

Well it's hard enough to love someone
When they're right close at home
Don't you think I know it's hard, honey
Squeezin' sugar from the phone

Guess the road is in my blood
Cause I'm my daddy's kid
You have to learn how to let me go
Just like my mama did

I got to go
I hope you'll understand
I love you so
Want you to be my man

I hear it call
Sounds so sweet and plain
I got to go, baby
'Cause the road's my middle name

Hear it call
And it sounds so sweet and plain
I got to go
'Cause the road is my middle name
I got to go
'Cause the road's my middle name
Ooh, I got to go, darlin'
Because the road is my middle name

## HAVE A HEART

*Words and Music by Bonnie Hayes*

Hey, shut up!  Don't lie to me
You think I'm blind but I've got eyes to see
Hey mister, how do you do?
Oh, pardon me, I thought I knew you
Would you stand back, baby
'Cause I want to get a better look
The big man who couldn't handle
The little bit of love you took

*Chorus:*
Hey, hey have a heart
Hey, have a heart
If you don't love me, why don't you let me go?
Have a heart
Oh, don't you have a heart?
Little by little you fade while I fall apart

Oh, oh, oh darling, I loved you so
I told you yes and then you told me no
Baby, how can you say
You should be free and I should pay and pay?
And you talk and talk
About you and what you need
But sooner or later
Your love is gonna make me bleed

*Chorus*

Oh, oh...

Talk on, talk on
But love is what you need
And sooner or later
That love is gonna make you bleed

*Chorus*

## TOO SOON TO TELL

*Words and Music by*
*Mike Reid and Rory Bourke*

So now there's somebody new
These dreams I've been dreaming
Have all fallen through
You say I'll be fine
It only takes time
Someday that may be true

But it's too soon to tell
Ah, it's too soon to say
Maybe someday I'll be able
To wish you well
But right now
It's just too soon to tell

It's all for the best, so you say
You never intended
To hurt me this way
You want to hear
I won't drown in my tears
Well, baby, the best that I can say

Is it's too soon to tell
Ah, it's too soon to say
Maybe someday I'll be able
To wish you well
But right now
It's just too soon to tell
Well, right now
It's just too soon to tell
Too soon to tell

## REAL MAN

*Words and Music by Jerry L. Williams*

Don't want no secret agent
Don't need no long Cadillac
I don't want nobody with no problems
I don't need a man with a monkey on his back

I want a real man
I said a real man
I need a real man
Ain't messin' with no toy
I don't need no baby boy

Don't need to send me no flowers, babe
Sending flowers is real nice
The way I've been feeling
My hearts been a-reeling
I need a man to love me once
I want a man to love me twice

It's a sticky situation, babe
Keep me up late at night
Honey, don't know the difference
You wanna go left when you shoulda gone right

I need a real man
I said a real man
I want a real man
I've been around the world
I'm a woman, not a girl

I don't want no million dollars
I don't need no diamond ring
You can twist and shout
Go on and knock yourself out
I don't care about material things

I want a real man
I need a real man
I want a real man
I said a real man
I want a real man
I need a real man
I want a real man
I want a real man
Real man

# THING CALLED LOVE

*Words and Music by John Hiatt*

Don't have to humble yourself to me
I ain't your judge or your king
Baby, you know I ain't no Queen of Sheba
We may not even have our dignity
This could just be a powerful thing
Baby, we can choose, you know we ain't no amoebas

*Chorus:*
Are you ready for the thing called love?
Don't come from me and you, it comes from up above
I ain't no porcupine, take off your kid gloves
Are you ready for the thing called love?

I ain't no icon carved out of soap
Sent here to clean up your reputation
Baby, you know you ain't no Prince Charming
Now we can live in fear, or act out of hope
For some kind of peaceful situation
Baby, how come the cry of love is so alarming?

*Chorus*

Ugly ducklings don't turn into swans
And glide off down the lake
Whether your sunglasses are off or on
You only see the world you make

*Chorus:*
Are you ready for the thing called love?
Don't come from me and you, it comes from up above
I ain't no porcupine, take off your kid gloves
Are you ready for it?
Are you ready for love, baby?
Are you ready for love, baby?

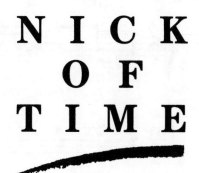

NICK
OF
TIME

# I AIN'T GONNA LET YOU BREAK MY HEART AGAIN

Words by David Lasley and Julie Lasley
Music by David Lasley

# THE ROAD'S MY MIDDLE NAME

Words and Music by Bonnie Raitt

'cause the road is my mid-dle name.

I got to go, 'cause the road's my middle name.

Oo, I got to go darlin', because the road is my mid-dle name.

Tacet

N.C.

38

# HAVE A HEART

Words and Music by Bonnie Hayes

*Additional Lyrics*

2. Oh darling, I loved you so.
   I told you yes and then you told me no.
   Baby, how can you say
   You should be free and I should pay and pay?
   And you talk and talk about you and what you need.
   But sooner or later your love is gonna make me bleed. *(To Chorus)*

3. *Instrumental (16 bars)*
   Talk on, talk on, but love is what you need
   And sooner or later that love is gonna make you bleed *(To Chorus)*

# TOO SOON TO TELL

Words and Music by
Mike Reid and Rory Bourke

46

# REAL MAN

Words and Music by Jerry L. Williams

48

## Additional Lyrics

3. It's a sticky situation, babe.
   Keep me up late at night
   Honey, don't know the difference.
   You wanna go left when you shoulda gone right. *(To Chorus)*

5. I don't want no million dollars.
   I don't need no diamond ring.
   You can twist and shout, go on and knock yourself out.
   I don't care about material things. *(To Chorus)*

# THING CALLED LOVE

Words and Music by John Hiatt

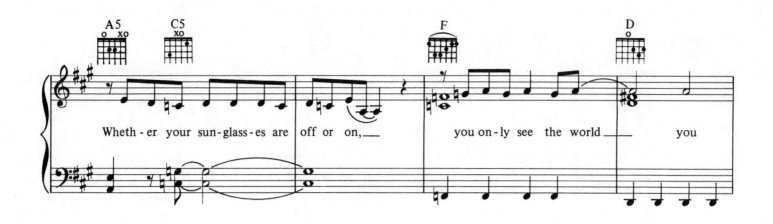

Wheth - er your sun-glass-es are off or on,___ you on-ly see the world___ you

make.

*D.S. al Coda*

Are you read-y for it? Are you read-y for the thing called love?___

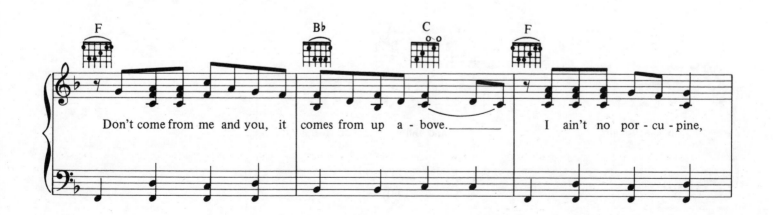

Don't come from me and you, it comes from up a - bove.___ I ain't no por-cu-pine,

# CHERRY LANE

## WHERE THE STARS OF TODAY SHINE!

**OASIS**
**Roberta Flack**
Roberta Flack is back! This matching folio includes ten new songs such as "All Caught Up In Love," "Uh-Uh Ooh-Ooh Look Out (Here It Comes)" and "Shock to My System."
CL#7949

**OTHER ROADS**
**Boz Scaggs**
Matching folio by one of the most respected artists in contemporary rock music. Songs featured are "What's Number One," "Heart of Mine" and "The Night of Van Gogh," plus a full color fold-out.
CL#7941

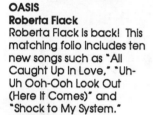

**AMNESIA**
**Richard Thompson**
The matching folio to one of England's most highly regarded rock n' rollers! Songs include "Turning of the Tide," "Gypsy Love Songs," "Jerusalem on the Jukebox" and more. Plus complete lyrics and photos.
CL#7946

**LET IT ROLL**
**Little Feat**
The matching folio to this great Southern rock band's latest album. Songs featured are the "foot stomping" tune "Cajun Girl" along with "Hate To Lose Your Lovin'" and "Voices In The Wind." Includes a full color fold-out and complete lyrics.
CL#7945

**SLOW TURNING**
**John Hiatt**
Following one of 1987's most acclaimed albums, this matching folio showcases the unique artistry of John Hiatt. Features the single "Slow Turning," plus "Paper Thin," "Drive South" and 9 more! Includes complete lyrics and photos.
CL#7942

**TILL I LOVED YOU**
**Barbra Streisand**
The hit album from one of the multi-talented singers of the twentieth century. Among the songs are the hit duet with Don Johnson, "Till I Loved You" as well as "What Were We Thinking Of" and "All I Ask Of You," from the Broadway sensation "Phantom of the Opera." Includes a full color fold-out and complete lyrics.
CL#7944

Catalogues are available upon request, please write to:
**CHERRY LANE MUSIC COMPANY, INC.**
**P.O. Box 430**
**Dept. BA**
**Port Chester, NY 10573**

Cherry Lane Music Company, Inc.
"quality in printed music"
P.O. Box 430, Port Chester, NY 10573-430